The Fireside Book 2021

"Friends should be like books – easy to find when you need them, but seldom used."
– Ralph Waldo Emerson

Contents

Poetry

From The Manse Window

iStock and Shutterstock.

Nature's Calendar

Illustrations by Sarah Holliday and Mandy Dixon.

Springtime Joys

WHAT are the joys of springtime?
Blossom buds, pink and white;
Baby birds cheeping from up in their nests
And day catching up with the night.

What are the joys of summer?
Paddling in cool, clear streams;
Lilies and roses and sunflowers, too,
And children devouring ice-cream!

What are the joys of autumn?
Leaves of orange and gold;
Succulent berries bursting with juice
And squirrels preparing for cold.

What are the joys of winter?
Hearing the north wind blow
Elegant branches on sleeping trees
And red-breasted robins in snow.

Lily Christie.

My Favourite Season

MANY years ago, when I was young,
I loved the autumn air:
The autumn with its eerie mists
That turned to droplets on my hair.

But now that I am growing old
It is the spring I love the best,
With new life burgeoning all around,
So joyous after winter's rest.

I love the promise springtime brings
When swathes of daffodils appear,
And daylight stretches more each day
And air is warmer, fresh and clear.

Perhaps we need the winter chill
In order that we all may treasure
The wonders that each new spring brings,
Which fill our lives with hope and pleasure.

Eileen Hay.

Visitors

THE sparrows squabble cheerfully;
The blackbirds are sedate.
The long-tailed tits arrive as one:
To watch them feels just great.

A sudden flash of colour
And a goldfinch lands nearby;
The chaffinch sings her happy song
From branches way up high.

The timid yellowhammers
Are so nice to have around.
They pick up all the birdseed
That's fallen on the ground.

The birds who choose to visit
My small garden for a while
Can always be relied upon
To raise a happy smile.

Chris Young.

My Bargain

I SAW it in the window:
On Sale, the ticket said.
It was the perfect lampshade
To hang above my bed.

I always like a bargain,
So in the shop I dashed.
I took it proudly homewards,
But oh, the colours clashed!

Yet still I loved my lampshade,
So what on earth to do?
Of course! I'd paint the bedroom
To match the lampshade's hue.

But now the rugs look awful,
And duvet, too, I fear.
Whoever guessed my bargain
Would cost me quite so dear!

Maggie Ingall.

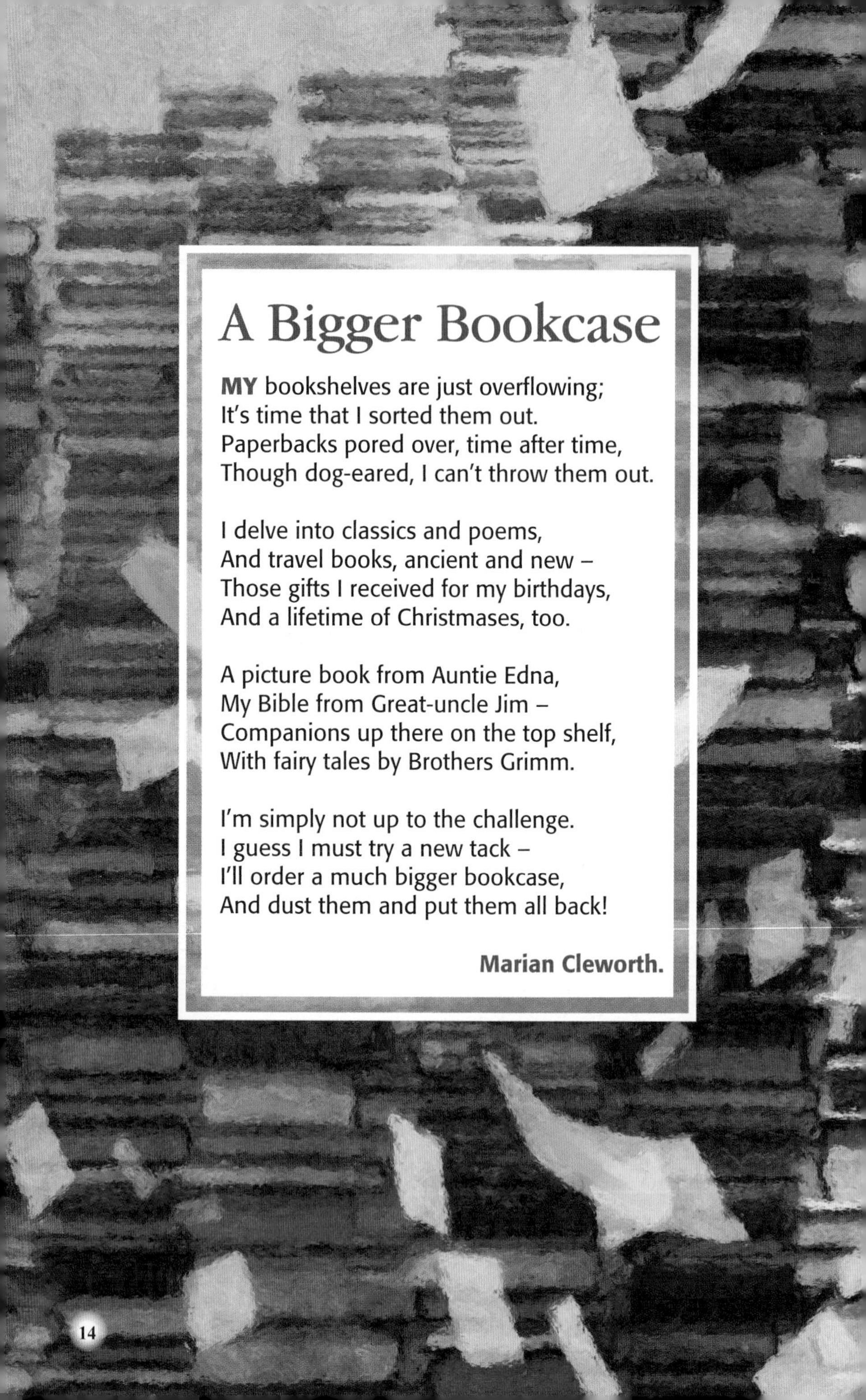

A Bigger Bookcase

MY bookshelves are just overflowing;
It's time that I sorted them out.
Paperbacks pored over, time after time,
Though dog-eared, I can't throw them out.

I delve into classics and poems,
And travel books, ancient and new –
Those gifts I received for my birthdays,
And a lifetime of Christmases, too.

A picture book from Auntie Edna,
My Bible from Great-uncle Jim –
Companions up there on the top shelf,
With fairy tales by Brothers Grimm.

I'm simply not up to the challenge.
I guess I must try a new tack –
I'll order a much bigger bookcase,
And dust them and put them all back!

Marian Cleworth.

from the Manse Window

A Doorway Into God

IN the words of the old music hall song, "I belong to Glasgow", and I am very proud to be a native of that wonderful, exciting city once described by the late Poet Laureate, Sir John Betjeman, as "the most beautiful Victorian city".

Rightly so, Glasgow is proud of its many parks. In fact, I once read that there are more parks in Glasgow than within any other British city.

Close to where I used to live, in the west end of the city, is Victoria Park. It's in this park that visitors will find Glasgow's most ancient attraction, the Fossil Grove.

The Fossil Grove is in essence a group of fossils discovered in 1887, and it contains the fossilised stumps and roots of 11 extinct Lepidodendron trees, with which aficionados will be well acquainted, I'm sure.

They were discovered after, in 1885, part of the Scotstoun Estate (the very area in which I was brought up) was leased to create a park.

The Fossil Grove was discovered a couple of years later when a pilot channel was cut through an old quarry in preparation for the construction of a road in the park.

It's reckoned that these remains are around 330 million years old – just a bit before our time – and today countless people come to see the famous Fossil Grove, which is situated within the Fossil House – a building constructed over the ancient relics to protect them from the elements.

While Glasgow's Fossil Grove is interesting and well worth a visit, no-one would say that these magnificent old relics are particularly beautiful.

However, these specimens alone are not the reason why so many thousands from all over the world visit the Fossil Grove.

The gardens and the fish pool there – situated in what was once a whinstone quarry – are breathtakingly beautiful, especially around springtime.

Around the small fish pool, on all the slopes and cliffs and in every nook and cranny, are

by Rev. Ian W.F. Hamilton

iStock.

flowers and bushes and trees in all their beauty, colour and splendour.

And it's right there in the heart of the city: banks of scarlet tulips and forget-me-nots, azaleas and rhododendrons bursting to life in shades of every hue.

As you would grasp the sheer loveliness of it all, I'm sure, like me, you would want simply to say "Thanks be to God." That's the effect its beauty had on a group of us some years ago.

While I was a divinity student at the University of Glasgow, I used to help lead an annual service in the Fossil Grove on the dawn of Easter Day, right there around the fish pool. The experience was nothing less than a springtime doorway into God.

There was once a poet who penned these words, "What can we cry, but glory be when God breaks out in an apple tree."

In so many ways my visits in the past to Glasgow's Fossil Grove have been doorways into God: the awesome magnificence of the ancient fossils, clearly the work of the Creator in the beginning, and the breathtaking beauty and splendour of the surrounding gardens.

Have you, in somewhat similar situations, ever suddenly been gripped by the same kind of feeling?

It happened once upon a time to Moses out in the desert in his encounter with a bush – a burning one! His life was transformed by that experience.

"The bush is on fire," he said, but he didn't just leave it at that, and simply go on to say, "How strange."

He didn't just pass by on the other side as most would have done, but rather, he said, "I must go across and see this wonderful sight!"

As the Old Testament records the story, Moses was a troubled man out there in the desert that day, and he was searching for purpose in his life.

Of necessity he had to leave a comfortable, privileged position in the Egyptian Court behind him because he had killed a man. He was now a fugitive in the desert.

But when he saw that bush, he saw much more than, as some have suggested, a fraxinella bush that gives off an inflammable oil which had ignited in the hot sun, or, as others have thought, a desert acacia bush ablaze with crimson flowers.

Moses looked with the eyes of faith and saw a divine splendour, and he heard God. For him it was the divine opening he was so desperately searching for – his doorway into God.

Perhaps you will have had your moments like that, too, when the ordinary has been lit up by the extraordinary, when God opened the door and suddenly surprised you – divine openings, that's what they are.

Of course it's not only through the experience of nature that our doorway into God can open, but certainly a springtime visit to the Fossil Grove in Glasgow's Victoria Park might just set your mind in motion and your heart ablaze, too. After all, "You are nearer God's heart in a garden, then anywhere else on earth."

So keep alert, wherever your travels may take you, for that burning bush in your life, that moment of truth, that divine "open sesame" – that doorway into God.

And when it opens, be gripped immediately by the moment, and be blessed abundantly by the one who said in parable to his hearers, "I am the door!" ■

iStock.

Nature's Calendar For Spring

An old German tale says the snowdrops lent their colour to the snow when none of the other flowers would.

The biggest tidal range in the world takes place in Canada, between Nova Scotia and New Brunswick in the Bay of Fundy. The range between high and low tide can be a staggering 16.3 metres, and you can see the results in the rock formation just off the coast.

Shutterstock.

A tradition similar to guising happens in Finland on the Sunday before Easter. Girls dressed up as witches go from door to door bringing blessings to drive away evil spirits – in exchange for treats, of course!

As the sun warms up, adders make an appearance again. Adders are some of the hardiest snakes in the world, living at up to 3,000 metres in the Alps and above the Arctic Circle.

Wild garlic grows in profusion in British woodlands, and can be picked for eating. The smell helps you identify it, and it's delicious processed with pine nuts, Parmesan and olive oil to make pesto.

Snowdrops In The Frost

I GATHERED coat and scarf and boots
And wrapped up with great care;
I'd been indoors for far too long
And needed some fresh air.
The cold was biting, razor sharp,
And nipped my ears and nose.
I felt my fingers growing numb
And couldn't feel my toes!
Head down, I trudged along the lane,
Then saw, to my delight,
A clump of snowdrops on the verge,
So fragile, pure and white.
The frost was glittering all around;
They trembled in the cold,
But there they grew, this hope of spring,
Defiant, brave and bold!

Eileen Hay.

Spring Again

SPRING has slipped her slippers off
And gently flutters through the air,
Touching trees that soon will leaf,
Bringing beauty everywhere.

The snowdrop lifts her lovely head
And others soon will join the ranks;
A verdant mantle clothes the ground
With cowslips seen 'midst grassy banks.

Softer winds begin to blow,
The earth refreshed with gentle rain
Will once again burst forth with life,
So pleased to see spring back again.

Megan Carter.

The Dawn Chorus

THE orchestra starts tuning up
As dawn begins to break,
And rays of light now tell the world
That it is time to wake.
The blackbird likes to lead the way,
Sounds swelling in his throat,
And then red-breasted robin adds
His rather wistful note.
That tiny feathered ping-pong ball,
The wren, now adds his trill,
Then blue tits, sparrows, finches join
And fill the air until
The sweetest singer of them all,
The song thrush, joins the choir,
And now their singing's at its peak,
Just soaring higher and higher.
I know they sing to find a mate
Or just defend their patch;
To me, it seems they sing for joy –
This choir that has no match.

Eileen Hay.

Hope And Cheer

SMALL bulbs that in the earth lie still,
While shepherds freeze on yonder hill,
Why wait unseen beneath the ground,
Forgotten till the day you're found?

Thrust up and show your trumpets high
On jaunty stalks, and seek the sky!
What sound comes from your yellow heads?
What whispered words of joy you spread!

The softly rustling sounds we hear
When crowded stems sway in the breeze,
Bring happy news of hope and cheer
Like nesting birds and busy bees.

James S. Stevenson.

Lambing Time

THE world is such a scary place
When you're a few hours old,
And wobbly legs won't hold you up
And the wind is, oh, so cold!

But very soon the bounce arrives
And legs are made of springs,
And you can rush around this world
That's full of wondrous things.

We love to watch lambs skip around,
Enjoying each twirl and leap,
But all too soon those frisky lambs
Become just staid old sheep!

Eileen Hay.

Mothering Sunday

GIVE thanks once more on Mother's Day
For mothers everywhere,
For all their help and comfort
And all their loving care.

For mothers who are out of sight,
We think of them today.
The memories will bring them close;
They're never far away.

Give thanks today for Mother Earth
And all each day can bring,
The plants and flowers, fields and trees,
The wonder of the spring.

Give thanks once more for Mother Church
And all the hope we find,
For love and healing, friendship, too,
And quiet peace of mind.

And so rejoice, lift up your hearts,
Go bravely on life's way.
Remember love, remember joy –
Give thanks on Mother's Day!

Iris Hesselden.

April Awakening

IT is the time when flowers raise their heads
In a bold brightness of yellows, purples, reds,
And the sun makes raindrops glisten on gossamer threads.

It is the time of lengthening and light,
Evenings become balmy, fragrant, bright,
And when the crickets chirrup in the night.

It is the time when birdsong meets the day,
A chorus carolling at dawn's first ray,
A million tuneful heralds trill and play.

It is the time when in the showers and the sun
A cycle new and ageless has begun,
The earth has turned, a battle has been won.

Deborah Mercer.

from the Manse Window

Keeping The Faith

"O WIND, if winter comes, can spring be far behind?"

I imagine quite a few of us have come across those famous words from Shelley's "Ode To The West Wind".

Although the question may not actually expect an answer, I'm afraid that, sometimes, at this time of year, my immediate mental retort is, "Yes, and it's a very long way behind!"

For who doesn't look forward to the arrival of spring?

Nothing lifts the spirits more than that first sight of new buds forming, of new shoots pushing bravely up through the earth.

Brighter days undoubtedly lead to lighter hearts!

Sadly spring, although arguably the most loved of all the seasons, is also the most capricious.

It loves to indulge in the game of "Now you see me, now you don't", when one day of sunshine can be followed by a week of leaden skies, chill rain and biting winds.

We know that, of course, spring will arrive sooner or later. Indeed, the Met Office can even offer us official start dates for both the meteorological spring and the astronomical spring.

But when morning after morning dawns gloomy and grey, it can take an effort of will to hang on to that hope of better times ahead.

Which is so often like life. Yet somehow people do manage to keep faith – even when their own particular wintry period looks as if it might never end.

We have so many heroes and heroines to look to for inspiration.

Like the late Professor Stephen Hawking who, even when told by doctors he was unlikely to live to his mid-twenties, persisted in his quest for scientific knowledge to the eventual benefit of us all.

Then there is J.K. Rowling who, as a divorced young mother living on benefits, continued to have faith in her writing despite a stream of publishers' rejections.

The results of her tenacity are the Harry Potter stories, enjoyed by all age groups and well known for coaxing reluctant

iStock.

by Maggie Ingall

children into becoming enthusiastic readers.

On the other side of the Atlantic we have Franklin Roosevelt. When, at the age of thirty-nine, he contracted the bout of polio which left him permanently paralysed from the waist down, he must have felt like despairing.

Yet he still found the courage to go on, eventually becoming the much-respected President of the USA.

Just as inspirational are the 10 athletes of the Refugee Olympic Team who competed in Brazil in 2016.

These sportsmen – who originally came from Ethiopia, Syria, the South Sudan and the Democratic Republic of the Congo – not only achieved a success that must have once seemed beyond their wildest dreams, but also, in doing so, have given new hope to thousands of other displaced young people.

It's important not to forget that such faith in a better future is not only to be found in high-profile examples.

I guess quite a few of us will have experienced times when we'd need a high-powered telescope to glimpse that light at the end of the tunnel.

With luck we can work through the darkness by ourselves – but with even more luck we will have someone to help us get there.

Which reminds me of Bill.

A few years ago he went through a bleak period. Not only was he made redundant from his office job, but the setback also coincided

iStock.

with the worse blow of losing his wife to the long-term illness she'd battled for years.

For a while, as he later acknowledged, "There seemed no point in going on with anything."

It was his friend Della who came to the rescue.

"She reminded me that, when I took over the household cooking duties some while ago, my wife told me I was good enough to be a professional.

"I knew that I enjoyed working with food and inventing my own recipes. So Della persuaded me that I should set up a small business, catering for parties and similar events."

Bill grinned.

"It seemed she was right," he said. "Orders quickly came in – so fast, in fact, that I wondered if I'd be able to keep up the pace!

"But it certainly gave me something positive to concentrate upon, not to mention some much-needed income.

"It was a great morale booster to find out that people liked what I did, and I was happy to be so busy.

"What I'd forgotten to take into account was that all this was happening in the run-up to Christmas. Once the festive season was over, things became suddenly extremely quiet."

He frowned in remembrance.

"I must confess that it was a big knock-back. Once again, I started to feel life was never going to get any better.

"But Della didn't give up on me. She remained so positive that things would eventually pick up that she kept my own faith going.

"Meanwhile, as she pointed out, the spare time would give me an excellent opportunity to practise some new recipes – and for inviting family and friends round to sample them.

"She found some quotes to encourage me – some of them funny, some serious, but all of them helpful."

His favourite came from Hal Borland.

"No winter lasts for ever; no spring skips its turn."

I'm pleased to report that Bill's friend was right, and that business did pick up, as did his spirits.

Not a world-changing achievement, admittedly, but one that nevertheless has changed Bill's life for the better, and which is also much appreciated by his many regular customers.

So, whether you are trying to get through this winter weather, or your own personal "winter", I wish you strength, courage and persistence.

Spring will come, after all, even if not always quite as speedily as we'd like it to! ■

Nature's Calendar For Spring

The seas put on a number of impressive bio-luminescent displays, but one of the loveliest takes place in Toyama Bay in Japan. Firefly squid appearing just before sunrise light up in mating season in late spring. Though they're just three inches long, it's quite a display.

Alamy.

The most common ladybird species in the UK is the seven-spot ladybird, though there are an incredible 47 species in the UK and over 5,000 around the world.

Shutterstock.

Over the course of its lifetime, the European rabbit can produce up to a staggering 360 offspring. The Norway lemming is just behind it with 192. Larger mammals like bears and tigers are between 15 and 20.

A spring onion is just a very young onion, picked after planting in autumn. They're a great source of vitamin C and calcium, and the sulphur in them can help lower your blood sugar level.

Gardeners often find themselves plucking out dandelions from flower-beds. However, they're actually a great native plant to grow, with highly nutritious leaves. Added to salads, they're an excellent source of vitamins A, C and K.

The Little Things

WHEN the sky is grey and heavy,
Seek a tiny patch of blue,
And when the earth lies cold and hard,
Just watch those shoots break through.

If sometimes you're downhearted,
It's time to share a smile,
For someone else is needing one
To make their day worthwhile.

And even when it's pouring down,
Still look for something bright.
Just see the florist's window bloom
With colour and with light.

So flow with nature, time and tide
And all tomorrow brings,
And counting blessings, look around,
Enjoy the little things!

Iris Hesselden.

A Window In The Rain

I FIND it quite evocative
To sit and watch the rain
Beat ceaselessly and timelessly
Upon the window-pane.

To mist the inside with my breath
And watch the world turn grey
As sweeping raindrops slowly leach
The colour all away.

I often feel nostalgic,
Remembering childhood days,
When I would sit for hours on end
And wistfully just gaze

At rain-soaked grass and dripping trees
And will the rain away,
So that the sunshine would appear
And I could run and play!

Eileen Hay.

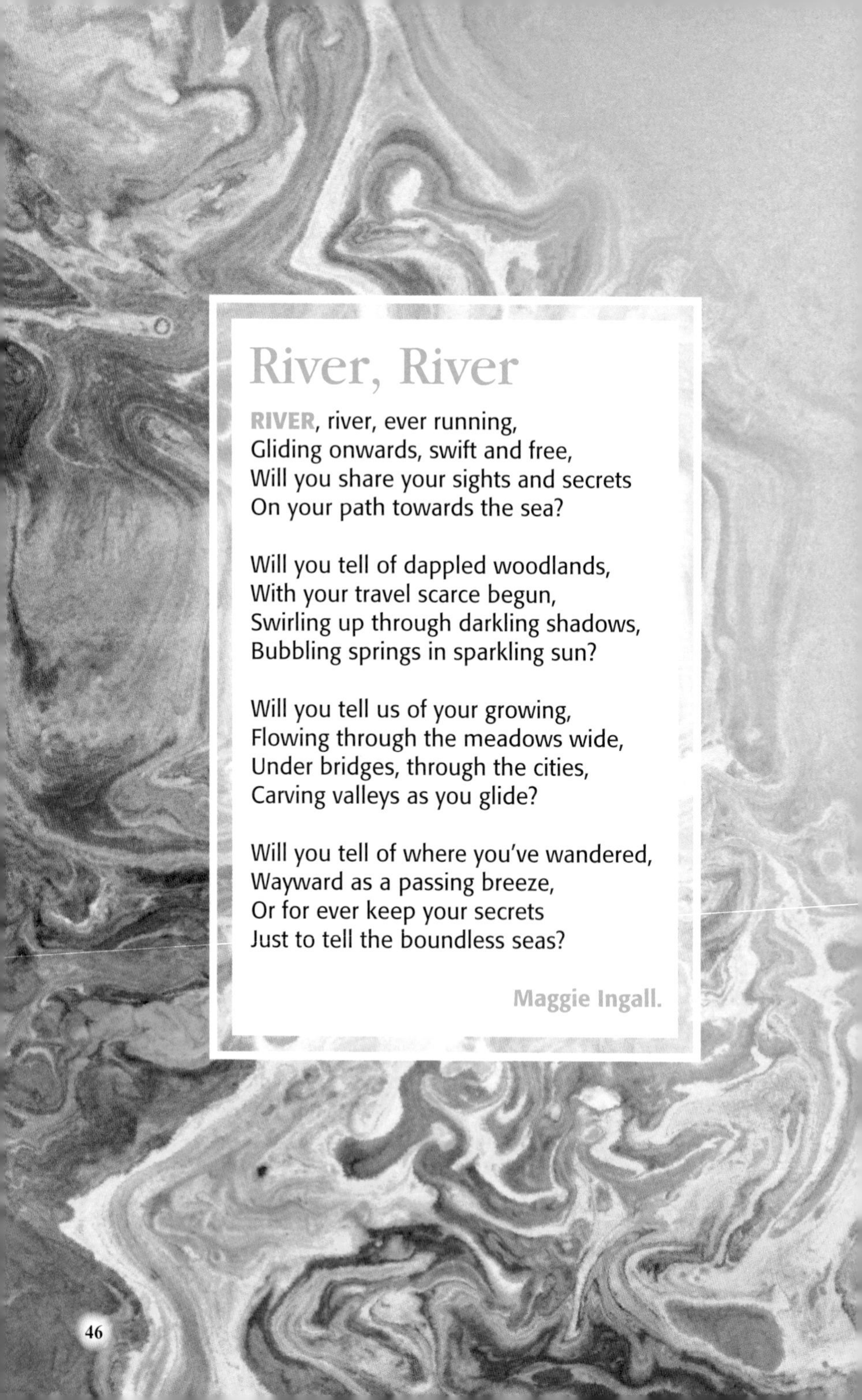

River, River

RIVER, river, ever running,
Gliding onwards, swift and free,
Will you share your sights and secrets
On your path towards the sea?

Will you tell of dappled woodlands,
With your travel scarce begun,
Swirling up through darkling shadows,
Bubbling springs in sparkling sun?

Will you tell us of your growing,
Flowing through the meadows wide,
Under bridges, through the cities,
Carving valleys as you glide?

Will you tell of where you've wandered,
Wayward as a passing breeze,
Or for ever keep your secrets
Just to tell the boundless seas?

Maggie Ingall.

Memories Of June

THE sleepy drone of bumblebees,
The cry of darting swifts,
Sweet honeysuckle's evening air:
June's constant summer gifts.

A sky that's brushed with feather clouds,
White shining on the blue;
Wind-painted patterns drifting by,
Our perfect evening view.

Hot noonday sun that burns the earth,
Tall trees that lend us shade;
Warm June nights when the moon is full:
These memories never fade.

Elizabeth Brown.

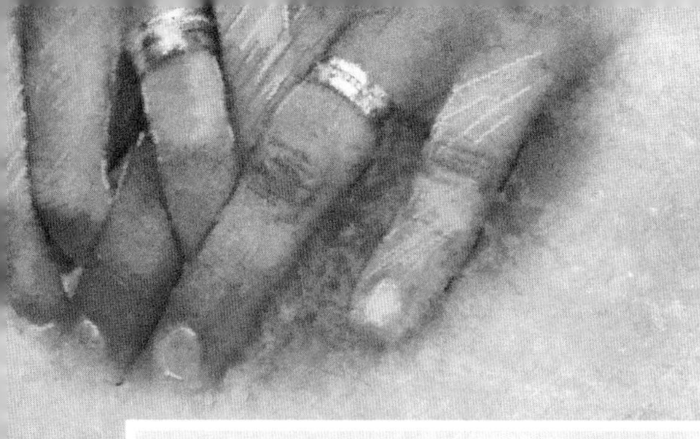

My Daughter's Hand

MY baby daughter's tiny hand, so delicate and slight,
She wraps it round my finger with her grasp so small and tight.
My trusting toddler's hand with its unquestioning small clasp,
Together we explore the world, each leaf, each blade of grass.

My busy schoolgirl's restless hand, it's there and then it's not,
She runs, she plays, she has such fun – we don't hold hands a lot.
My teenage daughter's growing hand, I rarely get to hold,
Unless she is upset and then my clutch is firm and bold.

My grown-up daughter's graceful hand, today she gives to you,
To crown it with a wedding ring, to show your love is true.
From today, her hand in yours, your lives will be together,
Please love, protect and cherish her, for now and for ever.

Lily Christie.

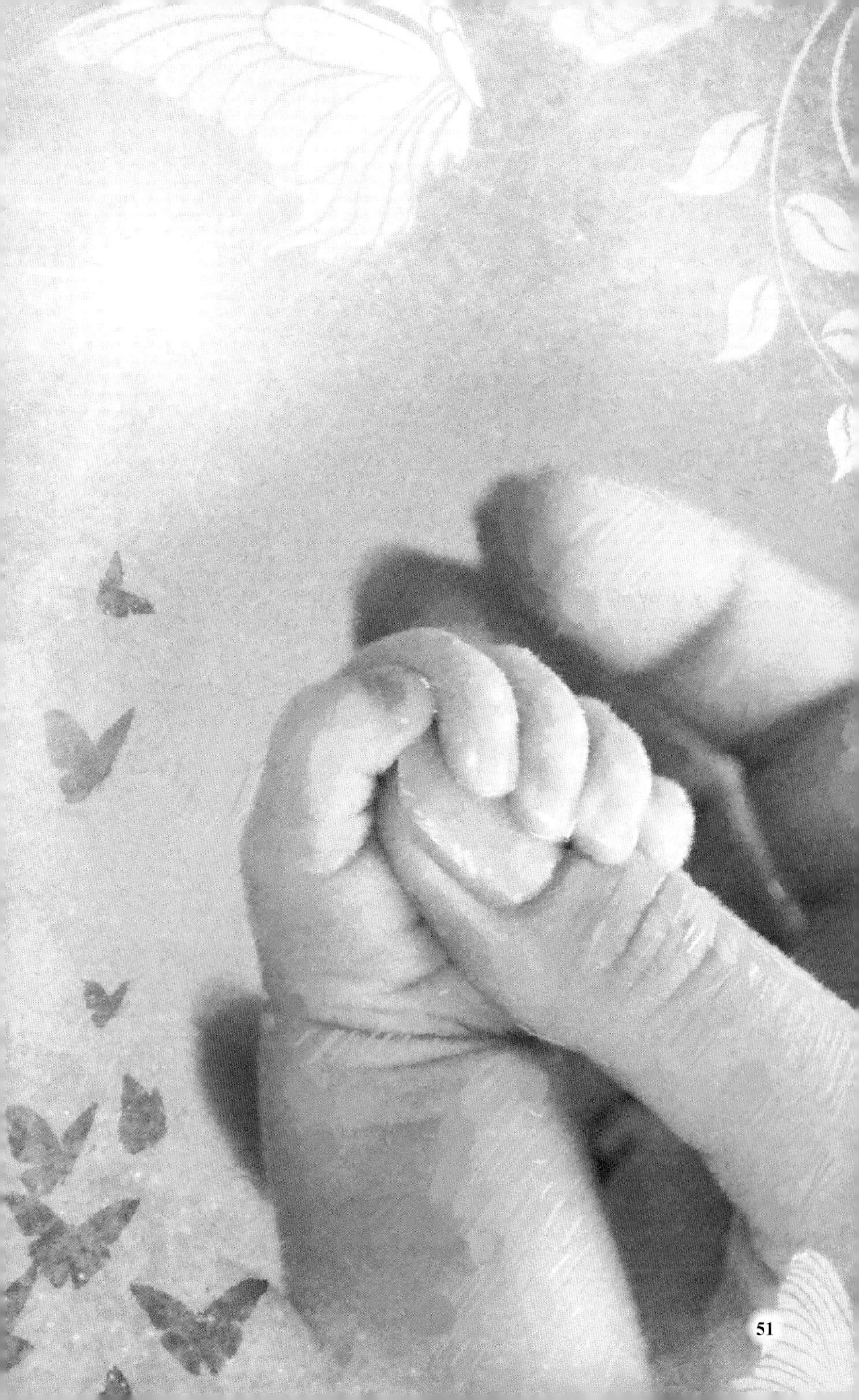

On Father's Day

TODAY is filled with memories
All gathered through the years,
With thoughts of Dad on Father's Day:
The laughter and the tears.
We think of times when we were small
And we walked hand in hand,
And though he didn't say a lot,
He seemed to understand.

Then as we grew and time slipped by
So many things we shared,
As we went rushing through our lives
We knew how much he cared.
And even though the years have flown
The bonds are strong and true,
Not just today, but every day,
Dear Dad, we think of you.

Iris Hesselden.

From The Footpath

ACROSS the meadow, if you look,
You'll see a ruined wall.
They say it was an abbey once
That stood there strong and tall.

Now willow herbs and nettles grow
Where grey-robed monks once trod,
Their plainsong stilled; it's skylarks now
Who send their praise to God.

I've heard that leaded glass once filled
That empty arch you see,
Yet now it frames a different view
Of grass and sky and sea.

It's getting dark, let's turn for home,
And leave this place to sleep,
For time runs like a river here,
Serene and slow and deep.

Maggie Ingall.

Escaping It All

WHAT a difference it makes to escape from it all,
If just for a day, maybe two,
Away from the humdrum routines of your life,
To visit old places and new.

To relax on a terrace and look out to sea,
As waves tumble on to the sand,
With the sun on your face and its warmth in your bones
And a book and a cool drink to hand.

No shrilling phone breaking into your thoughts
No knocks at the door now and then –
A chance to reflect on what matters the most
And come home refreshed once again.

Marian Cleworth.

from the Manse Window

Surprising Strength

IT was a vibrant summer's day. The world seemed bursting with colour and life and children could be heard playing in the distance. But I just wasn't feeling it.

I'm guessing we all have days like this from time to time. I would honestly have preferred to spend it slouched on the couch, feeling sorry for myself. But a wet tongue on the back of my hand eagerly insisted otherwise.

Dog owners, I was reminded, are not allowed lazy or self-indulgent days.

Boots on and doggy accoutrements collected, we set off, Zara and me. At least one of us was full of energy and excitement.

Thorn bushes briefly border one of the paths we walk as we leave the houses behind. I noticed a moth of some sort fly into one of the bushes, explore it, and fly out again safely.

How does it do that, I wondered. How do such soft fluttering wings avoid getting torn to pieces in such a jagged environment?

Perhaps their very softness was, in some way, a strength in that situation.

"A gentle answer turns away wrath," I muttered, quoting from Proverbs.

Perhaps the little creature's innate gentleness was an antidote to the "wrath" of the thorns.

We walked on to what had once been an industrial estate. The buildings had long ago been levelled and nature was doing a superb job of reclaiming the roads and the rubble. Foxes, frogs, deer and buzzards have all been seen there since the factories moved out.

Zara was following what might have been a rabbit track through long grass when I saw her jump a little to the side.

She briefly inspected what had startled her, then trotted on. I took a closer look.

A peacock butterfly had landed on a stalk of grass. Threatened by what might, for all it knew, have been a giant predator, it had resisted the instinct to try to fly away, spreading its wings

iStock.

by David McLaughlan

wide instead.

In theory, the bright colours on those beautiful wings act as a warning to anything that might want to eat it.

"I'm dangerous and not very tasty," the colours say. It's a survival technique.

Zara had gone and the butterfly relaxed. I wasn't up close and sniffing at it, so I was no threat.

When it relaxed, those wings rose vertically until they were straight up and leaning against each other.

The patterns and the colours on the tops of the wings had been fascinating, but the undersides were a dull brown. No distinctions, no patterns, just dull brown. People who propose such theories suggest this might be the butterfly's attempt at camouflage, making itself look like a dead leaf.

But, I wondered, always looking forward and down in search of the next flower as it flies, does the butterfly ever get to see how beautiful it is?

When relaxed, as I would have been on my couch, would it see itself as dull and uninteresting, as I had been tempted to see myself? And if it does see the topsides of those wings, could it possibly understand our concept of beauty and how it seems to us, looking down from above?

I fleetingly imagined God laughing – or perhaps it wasn't my imagination.

"I get it, Lord," I replied. "How I'm feeling today, how I'm seeing myself, is like the underside of the butterfly's wings. You see me from above."

I dug a tennis ball from my pocket and the rest of the walk was a good deal more energetic. One throw of the ball went further than I anticipated.

Strong, I thought.

My mind turned back to the moth in the thorn bush. I imagined Jesus in the garden at Gethsemane, confronted by Judas and "a crowd armed with swords and clubs". A "thorny" situation, indeed!

He could, undoubtedly, have taken the strong way, but strength wasn't important at that point. There was another, better way to go.

Because he still had a message to proclaim, he took the gentle way, rebuking his disciple who wanted to fight thorns with thorns. The gentle – weak – way was, in itself, an important part of his message.

I once saw an electron microscope photo of a moth's wing. It isn't a smooth surface as you might imagine. It is actually full of holes. So much so, it's a wonder the creature can fly.

All those holes make the wings lighter, more flexible, but wouldn't they also make them weaker?

Surely, I thought, wings work by pushing against the air. They need to be strong. The air would go right through those.

But it doesn't. Because the holes are tiny, air going into them causes turbulence, which effectively blocks them and prevents any more air from following, giving the effect of a completed surface.

If the holes weren't there, the wings would be too heavy and rigid for the little guy to move. But they are there so the moth gets lightness and flexibility, plus all the strength of solid wings, by having wings that are weaker and softer.

There is so often, as those wings show us, surprising strength in softness. And so often, as the peacock butterfly's wings showed me, surprising beauty behind ugliness.

Needless to say, by the time we returned home we had a very different attitude towards ourselves and the day. We had been reminded of how God sees us all and the intricate mastery of his grand design, which is bound to lift anyone's spirits to the point where they might feel they could fly.

I say "we" – I'm pretty sure Zara was already tuned into all of that. Our animal cousins so often are. It's usually us humans who need the reminding. And the best reminder of all is often a simple walk through God's Creation. ■

iStock.

Nature's Calendar For Summer

Between April and September the sun is in the right position to shine into the Enchanted Well in Brazil's Chapada Diamantina National Park. The water is up to 40 metres deep, and is so clear that you can see straight to the bottom.

The chances of seeing a badger increase during the summer as there's often a bit of light left when they come out to forage. They live in large family groups with multiple rooms in their setts. The biggest in Britain was over 15 x 35 metres with 12 entrances!

Shutterstock.

Every year in North America's picturesque Smoky Mountains, tens of thousands of fireflies – known as lightning bugs – gather for an extremely rare display of synchronous light. The whole swarm flashes in harmony and people can buy tickets to see the display. Two thousand different species of bio-luminescent beetles exist, but few synchronise like this.

There's a giant stone at the top of the mountain that Machu Picchu is built on which not only lines up perfectly with the spring and autumn equinoxes, but also has four corners which point perfectly in the four directions of the compass.

Boiling nettles removes the sting from them, and then they can be used for teas and soups, amongst other things. Don't wait until they're mature, as the leaves are hard on the stomach – it's the youngest leaves that are best.

A Cup Of Tea

ON days when it was stifling hot
And I came in from play,
My aunt would put the kettle on –
And this is what she'd say:

"A cup of tea is what I need
To help to cool me down."
But I asked "Why?" and shook my head,
Then added with a frown,

"I need a drink that's nice and cold.
Some water – that will do.
How can you cool with something hot?
I'm not as mad as you!"

My aunt just laughed and mopped her brow,
Then poured herself more tea.
"It's said that hot drinks cool one down –
Just try, and then you'll see."

I couldn't make much sense of it,
But now I find it's true;
The experts all confirm it
As a helpful thing to do.

Although it sounds an old wives' tale,
Old tales don't always fool.
Try a cup of warming tea
To help to keep you cool!

Dawn Lawrence.

Seaside Memories

SO many seaside memories,
Such pictures they all make,
So many things forgotten –
You've stirred them all awake.
The patient donkeys on the beach,
They wait for me and you,
And lovely sticks of coloured rock
That have the name all through.
Some sweets that look like pebbles
And rock that looks like fruit,
With canvas shoes and green sunshades
And hats that look so cute.
Along the shore a crowd appears,
There's Punch and Judy now,
And then a clown has just arrived
And stops to take a bow.
Do you remember if it rained?
I only see the sun,
And life had laughter, love and joy
With innocence and fun.
So many happy seaside days –
Has all the magic died?
But no, we'll keep it safely stored
To warm us, deep inside!

Iris Hesselden.

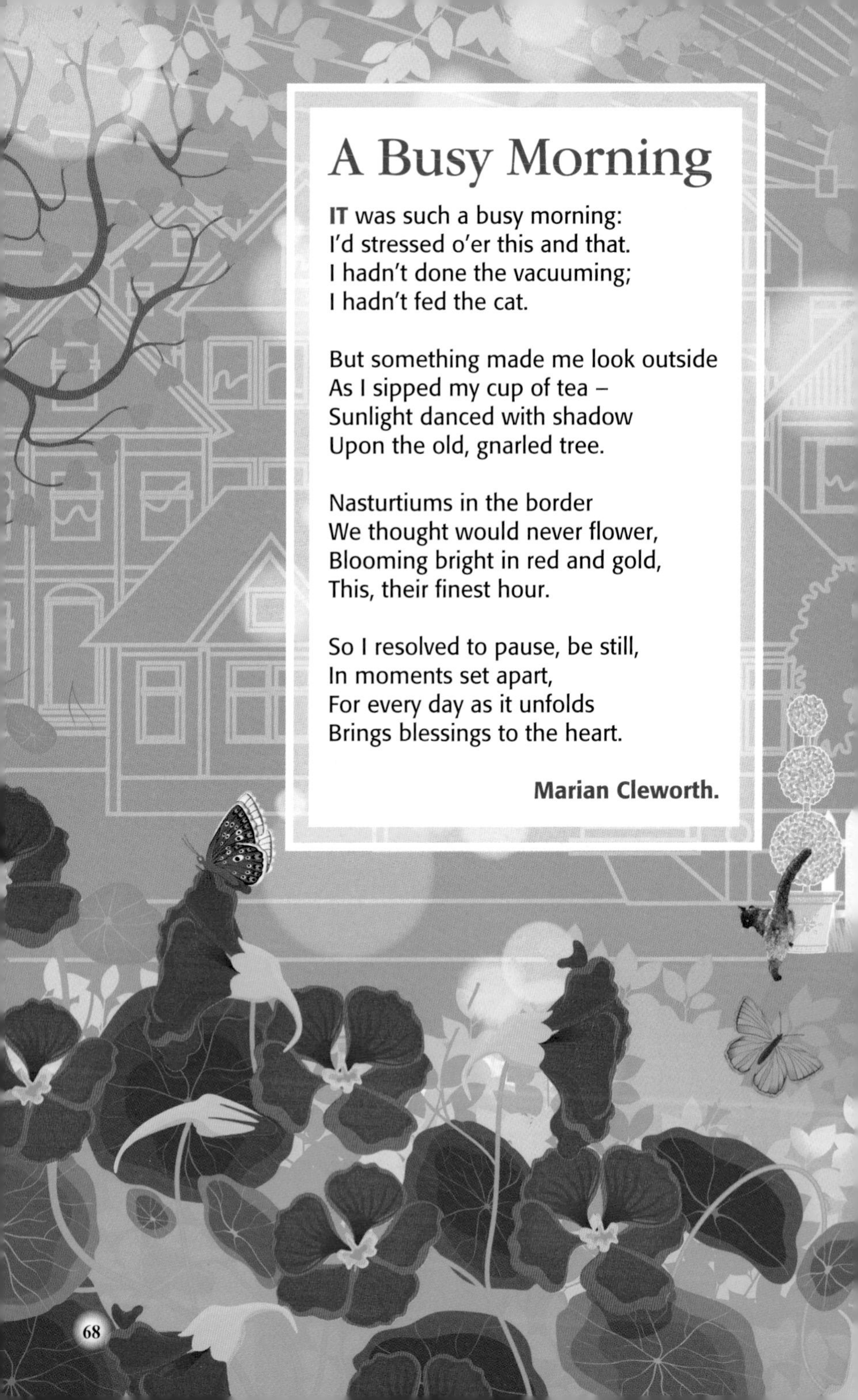

A Busy Morning

IT was such a busy morning:
I'd stressed o'er this and that.
I hadn't done the vacuuming;
I hadn't fed the cat.

But something made me look outside
As I sipped my cup of tea –
Sunlight danced with shadow
Upon the old, gnarled tree.

Nasturtiums in the border
We thought would never flower,
Blooming bright in red and gold,
This, their finest hour.

So I resolved to pause, be still,
In moments set apart,
For every day as it unfolds
Brings blessings to the heart.

Marian Cleworth.

The Sound Of Bells

THE bell on the counter pings shiny and bright,
Demanding attention when no-one's in sight.
The bells at the church peal, tumbling and gay,
In celebration of a wedding day.
The bell at the school is strident and shrill,
Emptying playgrounds as classrooms fill.
Ships on the high seas have solid brass bells,
Signalling duty times and "All is well".
And from the reservoir comes the ghostly, chill sound
Of the bells from a village long since drowned.
They intone long and low in times of death;
They inspire great joy in times of birth.
Now there's a bell to tell the cake is done,
The washing is washed and an e-mail has come.
They signal our lives in so many ways,
As they did yesterday, today and always.

Thea Morgan.

Cameo

I HAD a dream – a dream that I must tell
Of sun and sand, of ocean's salty spray,
Some treasured shells, a crab, a shallow pool,
The breeze that stirred the sultry heat of day.

Those rising cliffs, the seagulls in their flight,
The white-sailed yacht, and vivid blue of sky;
Each ebb and tide, each breaker's noisy boom
And carefree joy of children milling by.

I had a dream – and oh! It seemed so real,
But now in morning light it fades away,
Yet who can tell that if I close my eyes
My dream will not return another day?

Elizabeth Gozney.

A Summer Meditation

LET me take you gently sailing –
Sailing on a river blue,
Leaving troubled thoughts behind us,
Find a peaceful, sunlit view.

Green and lovely summer meadows,
Cattle grazing, all is still.
In the distance, see a steeple
Sitting high upon the hill.

Round a bend, the river curving,
Now reveals a stately home,
Grand and warm and welcoming –
Who would ever want to roam?

Soon the river will be wider,
Reaching out towards the sea;
We must turn and go no further,
Turning back to field and tree.

Back through sunlit countryside,
Peace and quiet still our goal.
Take this calm serenity –
Let it fill your heart and soul.

Iris Hesselden.

The Garden

LABURNUM with its golden glow,
Ceanothus with its blue;
Lilac white and purple,
With the sunlight shining through.

Orange blossom, honeysuckle,
Stocks and mignonette;
Delphiniums and hollyhocks –
All names you won't forget.

Sunflowers and choisya,
With hibiscus bold,
Interspersed with roses,
Red and white and gold.

Wallflowers lining garden paths,
Jasmine draping walls;
Clematis hanging from the trees
In copious waterfalls.

Buttercups, marsh marigolds,
Ox-eye daisies, cowslips, too;
I gaze across the garden
Till the magic dims the view.

And add to this the birdsong,
The sight, the smell, the scent,
And think, where else can there be found
A cause for more content?

Dawn Lawrence.

from the Manse Window

Busy Doing Nothing

AFTER a week of summer squalls and showers, it was wonderful to wake up to blue skies and bright sunshine.

With the weather forecast promising a settled spell, I could think of no better way to celebrate than by taking a trip to the seaside.

Refreshed by a paddle and a strawberry ice-cream, I was idly examining a rack of postcards when something else caught my eye. It was on a nearby stand of souvenir fridge magnets.

There were pretty magnets and novelty ones, while others were humorous, but one in particular made me laugh aloud.

It bore the motto, *It may look like I'm doing nothing, but in my head I'm quite busy.* A defence that many of us could use, I suspect!

But as I wandered away, those words stayed in my mind. The more I thought about it, the stranger it seemed that we humans do seem to feel the need to defend ourselves whenever we don't appear to be Doing Something Useful.

Even if we don't actually rationalise the thought, it's as if we need to declare ourselves to the world.

"Hey, look at me, without me attending to it, this job might never get done. See how indispensable I am!"

You know, I can think of no other creature on earth that seems to feel the urge to prove that it's busy with some necessary task. Even animals are more sensible.

We see our cats or dogs lazing in the sun without it ever occurring to us that they ought to be doing something more constructive. Beasts, birds and mammals happily rest whenever they choose to – yes, even if it isn't actually bedtime!

Indeed, the sloth is famous for having turned the skill of doing nothing into an art form. And I do regard it as a skill.

I am not the first one, of course, to observe that too much busyness in our lives can end

iStock.

by Maggie Ingall

up being counterproductive. Simply working or worrying ourselves into a tizzy is never helpful.

We all need to let our brain take some downtime in order to process thoughts and experiences at its own pace as, just like recharging a battery, it will function all the better for it.

By not demanding instant action, we allow ourselves to properly mull over all options, and work out what is likely to succeed for us. Sadly, I don't suppose I'm the only person to have sometimes regretted acting with more haste than wisdom.

It's interesting to note that scientific studies confirm that the benefits of being idle are both real and measurable.

To begin with, inactivity can get our imaginations working and improve our creativity.

One research project, in which volunteers were asked to perform the mind-numbing task of copying down lists of phone numbers, revealed that boredom quickly prompted them to find all sorts of inventive ways to make the job more interesting.

Such findings do make sense as, after all, good ideas can only come to us if we've made the mental space for them.

Similar insight, if only we can recognise it, is given to us early by many authors of books aimed at children.

iStock.

"Don't underestimate the value of Doing Nothing, of just going along, listening to all the things you can't hear, and not bothering," A.A. Milne, author of the Winnie-the-Pooh stories, advised.

And in Kenneth Grahame's "The Wind In The Willows", it's only when Mole stops to rest quietly by the riverbank that the river "chattered on to him, a babbling procession of the best stories in the world, sent from the heart of the earth to be told at last to the insatiable sea".

What a lot Mole would have missed if he had been marching briskly from A to B, intent on getting there as soon as possible!

Such quotes could have provided encouragement for Hazel when she broke her ankle. It wasn't too bad a break, but nevertheless required a lot of rest if it was to mend properly.

As someone who was always busy, Hazel found it hard at first.

"It was only slowly that I learned to stop fretting, and start appreciating all the things that I never usually had time for," she admitted.

"For example, it wasn't until I was forced to sit still that I noticed how many birds visited our garden, and all the different kinds of insect life that enjoyed the plants and flowers.

"And when my grandchildren came to visit, I had time to listen properly to all their news and adventures, and even tell them stories about my own childhood. I wouldn't have chosen to break my ankle, but it certainly helped me to understand that being around is every bit as important as rushing around."

It's a shame that, for most of us, it does indeed take incapacity or illness to make us stop and appreciate the moment.

"Some of us need to discover that we will not begin to live more fully until we have the courage to do and see and taste and experience much less than usual.

"And for a man who has let himself be drawn completely out of himself by his activity, nothing is more difficult than to sit still and rest, doing nothing at all. The very act of resting is the hardest and most courageous act he can perform," Thomas Merton, the Trappist monk, writer and poet noted.

I believe that it does take courage to risk allowing others, and just as importantly, ourselves, to see that our constant busyness is not actually essential to keep the world spinning on its axis.

In fact, rather the opposite, for if we could all take more moments to be still and appreciate its many wonders, we might all be inspired to take a little more care of it.

Enjoy the summer sunshine if you can, and if you can't – well, even squalls and showers can bring rainbows to pause and marvel at! ■

Nature's Calendar For Summer

The world's largest bumblebee – Bombus dahlbomii – lives in the southern half of South America. The queen of the species grows up to 40 mm (1.6 in) in length.

The Chanthaburi Fruit Fair in Thailand takes place in an area known for its gemstones. Exotic fruits like durians, mangosteens and rambutans are all on display in competing arrangements. Thousands of fruit and veg are used during the celebrations.

Shutterstock.

Elderflowers are one of the most versatile natural ingredients still readily available in the countryside. They can be made into everything from cordials, jams and wines to skin lotions. You can even eat the flowers as they are, or add them to salads, though the leaves and stems are poisonous.

The Lut Desert in Iran is thought to hold the record for the hottest place on earth after reaching 70.7 deg. C. in 2005.

At the other end of the year from their winter hibernation, bears will now be roaming around and spending up to 20 hours a day eating. In some places, though, the bears have been struggling as unseasonably hot northern summers have damaged fish stocks.

Familiar Scenes

IT'S just a sleepy village, with a church, a school, a pond,
And tiny olde worlde cottages, with spreading hills beyond;
Where birds sing in the tree-tops, and the air is fresh and bright;
Where the flowers' fragrance lingers in the sunbeams' golden light.

The views are there to beckon, through the winding country lanes,
'Midst a briefly passing shower, of the summer's cooling rains;
Then towards a friendly cottage, for refreshing cups of tea,
Where the drift of new bread baking brings a childhood memory.

It's just a sleepy village, with familiar scenes so dear,
To feel a sense of coming home: of drawing ever near;
To reach out for the welcome, that the heart will always yearn,
And to find it warmly waiting for the traveller's return.

Elizabeth Gozney.

Waiting For A Train

BETWEEN summer showers, we explore leafy paths
Then shelter in the station by the narrow-gauge track.
Everything here has been tended with care:
Lavender, lobelia, geraniums everywhere.
On the tall bank opposite, young oaks filter light;
Ferns wave and birds chatter, out of our sight.
Then we hear the whistle of the engine's approach,
Echoing in the valley; she and her sisters all lovingly restored:
Their days in slate quarries a century ago,
A distant memory in the air, fading like smoke.

Rebecca Holmes.

Wilderness

I'VE strayed away from well-worn tracks,
I've journeyed far and wide.
The grass is soft beneath my feet;
A stream has been my guide.

But now it's time to rest awhile
And listen to the sound
As breezes tease the leaves on trees
And birds sing all around.

My seat is just a grassy knoll,
But like a throne to me,
Where I can sit in wonderment
At feeling really free.

This place is like a paradise
And I would love to stay,
But that old stream is calling me
To be back on my way.

Dennis W. Turner.

autumn

Song Of Autumn

THE summertime has slipped away;
The days went by so fast,
But they have left us happy thoughts
And memories to last.

But now the air feels different,
A fresh touch on the breeze,
And see those colours, red and gold,
There's magic in the trees.

The clouds are swiftly travelling,
They're scurrying along,
Now let the sunshine lift your heart
And share an autumn song!

Iris Hesselden.

The Antiques Shop

IT'S just an old antiques shop,
Rather dusty, rather small.
It has no rare, important things,
No priceless works at all.
Yet still I like to prowl its nooks,
Inspect its well-filled shelves,
To see what folks have left behind
To tell us of themselves.
So who, I muse, once stitched that screen?
Who worked that spinning wheel?
I look around and wonder
Just what secrets they conceal.
Who used that desk?
Who wore that brooch?
Who owned "A Young Man's Guide"?
Imagination fills the gaps
The objects can't provide.
And, though, of course, I'll never know
If what I guess is true,
It's still a game I love to play,
And maybe you might, too.

Maggie Ingall.

Transition

ALL the garden's glories now
Are wrapped in autumn's cloak,
While floating mists entwine themselves
With drifts of scented smoke.
Russet leaves, white-diamond clad,
Are draped in cobweb lace
As September comes a-wooing
With sweetly mellow grace.
Though days may still be gilded
As summer hugs and clings,
The skies spell out a sad farewell
Writ by departing wings.

Tricia Sturgeon.

The Artist

WHO is this secret spinner
Working in the mist,
Creating webs of magic,
Of gold and amethyst?
Someone who wakes so early
When the grass is wet with dew,
And carries on so tirelessly
To work the whole day through;
The work is never-ending,
But it's never grey or plain;
It shimmers with the dewdrops
And dances in the rain;
The spinner, though so cunning,
Might be someone you know well,
But since no-one has seen her,
There is no-one who can tell.

Dawn Lawrence.

Grandma's Pantry

TO us it was Aladdin's cave,
A treasure trove of all things good
Like still-warm bread and home-made jam
(Our truly all-time favourite food).

On higher shelves were rows of jars
Packed full of peaches, plums or pears
And, on the floor, a strange array
Of weird and wondrous iron wares

Whose purpose no-one really knew
(Though Grandma said, of course, she did),
And one huge marble slab for meat
That had a shiny wire mesh lid.

She had brass scales with different weights
And battered cans for paraffin,
Old mousetraps, moulds for jelly treats,
And pastry cutters in a tin.

I miss that pantry from my youth,
Our special little hideaway,
But still I have the memory
For ever safely tucked away.

Eileen Hay.

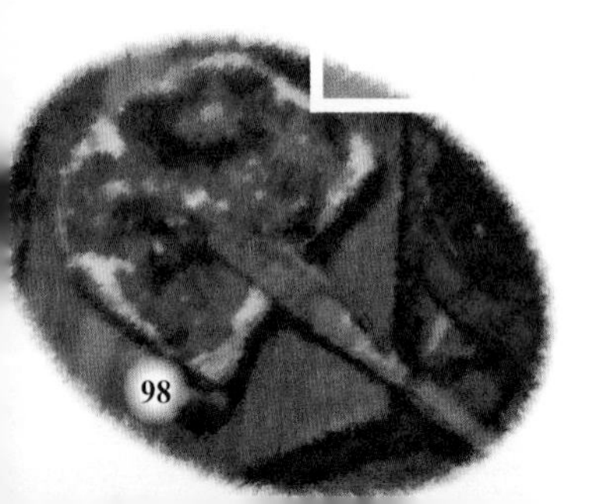

from the Manse Window

Shine Bright

DO I use beauty products? As an older man it would once have been a safe bet that I absolutely didn't. Times have changed.

However, I am almost certain I have never used any sort of dermal abrasion. Those are the various treatments for removing surface-level skin cells. Sometimes it has a medical purpose, but sometimes it's for the fresh, youthful glow that comes from exposing new skin.

Why was I even wondering? Well, I was on the beach on a dry but blustery day. The sand was flying.

Squinting, I turned my face from the beautiful Clyde estuary towards the ancient sea wall.

Fairlie sits in a narrow strip between the coast and the hills. Good sea defences would have been important from very early on.

The walls are substantial constructions, and although I am sure they have been weathered and damaged, for the most part they still stand firm.

My attention was caught by a white stone slab set just above head height. While the grandchildren explored rockpools, I took a closer look.

Something had been carved there once. Hints of letters could still be made out.

But who knows how many decades of crashing waves and wind-blown sand had "dermally abraded" the monument? What had once been written in stone had almost been wiped away.

Thankfully, there was a replacement: a large black plaque fixed to the wall just feet away. The original words had been recreated there. It seems the early inhabitants of the town hadn't just relied on the strength of the wall for their defence – they had also added some Scripture.

Even in the raging of the sea, it read, *thy mighty power doth reign. Billows sent, mountain-high, by thee are stilled by thee again.*

Wonderful. But the new plaque had another message for me.

Many years before, on the same stretch of coast, I had stumbled upon a sea

iStock.

by David McLaughlan

baptism. Curiosity had drawn me to the crowd. There, I went from being a casual onlooker to carrying the minister's clothes and towel.

As the woman who had just been baptised returned to shore, we all sang "Amazing Grace". It was a beautiful moment.

Then I got talking to one of the men. I explained how faith was a relatively new walk for me.

"Ah!" he said, wagging a finger in my face. "You have that look about you."

That look? What did he mean? Should I expect that feeling – that look – to fade?

I thought of the words of the song we had just sung: "When we've been there ten thousand years, bright shining as the sun."

Perhaps in heaven we can shine brightly for ten thousand years, but here on earth it seems we ought to expect to fade, to naturally suffer some dermal abrasion.

Perhaps he wasn't wrong. I found it a little disheartening, but that's the world for you.

But the good people of Fairlie hadn't settled for natural deterioration. They had renewed the message on the wall.

It occurred to me that we build our walls, towns and churches as a comfort against the immensity of time. But they inevitably fall again. The very best we can do is proclaim a message that outlasts them all. And when that message grows dull, we renew it.

"Do not conform to the patterns of this world, but be transformed by the renewing of your mind," Paul said in his letter to the Romans.

He told the Colossians to "put on the new self which is being renewed in knowledge in the image of its Creator".

Renewal is the way of nature, the way creation works. For everything that gets worn down, something else rises in glory. The problem comes when we get worn down – and stay down. When we lose "that look" and don't bother finding it again.

Renewal might come through reading the Bible; it might be fired up by new preaching, new experiences. Some people have perfected the knack of seeing each day as a brand-new and exciting gift.

Me?

"Papa!" Six-year old Nathan had his jacket zipped up and his hood pulled tight, but the weather was in no way diminishing his fun.

He had found an old iron ring set into a rock, once a mooring point for a boat, and wanted to know what would open up if we pulled or twisted it.

Four-year-old Evie, oblivious to her hair whipping around her, handed me a collection of stones and asked me to keep her "mermaid treasure" safe for her.

The heart-filling wonder of children is that they are seeing almost everything for the first time. They haven't had time to be bored by anything.

Expectation or familiarity have not yet dulled their experience. They are seeing creation as it really is. And they are almost always fascinated and amazed by it.

They are the renewal of my heart and soul. They are what wash away the accretions of time, the dead skin cells. They carve their experiences into my life in sharp-edged, freshly written letters.

It is little wonder Jesus said, "The Kingdom of God belongs to such as these." We have only to ask – God and the children – and we will be allowed in.

Shining bright in heaven after ten thousand years won't be difficult – it will be a gift by the grace of God. What is difficult – and is a big part of the work of faith – is to shine as bright in this world, and to keep that shine despite everything the world does to dull it down.

If you once had "that look", as my friend on the beach called it, and you would like it back, I have good news for you. It's yours for the asking.

It might come in "billows sent mountain high", it might come through the laughter of children and the warming of your heart, but it will come.

Break the patterns of this world. Beautify your soul. Be renewed! ■

iStock.

Nature's Calendar For Autumn

In Colombia, the Caño Cristales river runs for 100 km and has a huge diversity of sub-aquatic plants. In late summer to early autumn, local plant species on the riverbed become colourful, leading to the river's name of "River of Five Colours" or the "Liquid Rainbow".

Grey seals head to rocky shorelines to give birth as autumn nears. After a summer of rich pickings, the seals should hopefully be in good condition for the challenges ahead. After only two to three weeks, the pups make their own way in the world.

Shutterstock.

Mushrooms are a type of fungi, which can count themselves the largest living organisms on earth. Underground networks of fungi can extend up to three miles in length, creating connections between entire woodlands.

As they enter their busiest season of the year, squirrels actually get smarter during autumn. Studies show there's an average increase of 15 per cent in the size of their hippocampus – the part of the brain responsible for memory.

In coffee shops around the country, pumpkin spice starts appearing on the menu as the leaves fall, but it's nothing to do with pumpkins. It's a combination of cinnamon, ginger, nutmeg, cloves and allspice.

A Falling Leaf

I SEE the leaf fall to the ground,
Hover, pause, and spin around,
Then, with no option, flutter down,
Red and gold turned into brown.

Its edges crisp, its colours dim,
Caught on the breeze, I see it spin,
But it has no choice at all,
For it is autumn: it must fall.

It's lost the golden glow it had,
I watch it fall, am pensive, sad,
Others will follow in a throng –
It will not be alone for long.

And soon, where once green leaves were there,
The tree will rise up stark and bare,
And all the leaves that fluttered round,
Will disappear into the ground.

And then, unseen by us, below,
Blanketed by frost and snow,
They will nourish, feed the soil;
Nature's thrifty, does not spoil

What it nourished in the spring,
The leaf that once seemed dead will bring
New growth and life – I won't feel grief,
As I see the falling leaf.

Deborah Mercer.

The Dormouse

I'M someone secretive and small;
You'll hardly know I'm there at all,
But one day, should you get a chance
To catch a glimpse, a fleeting glance,
With whiskers brushed and eyes shut tight
I make a most appealing sight.
And when you see my fluffy tail,
To love me you can hardly fail;
I wrap it neatly round my head
Then curl up in my cosy bed.
In Britain, I'm the only kind
Of rodent very hard to find
In wintertime, because, you see,
No rodent hibernates like me.
But there's one creature I can name
Who, though he does not share my fame,
Looks and acts a lot like me
And is a special rarity.
The smallest mouse of any kind –
The little harvest mouse, you'll find.
And just like me, his nest he weaves
So cleverly from grass and leaves.
One has to search most patiently
To catch a glimpse of him – or me.

Dawn Lawrence.

The Sunken Village

THE streets where once the children played –
A normal, mundane, happy scene –
And mums with pushchairs stopped to chat
Are gone, as if they'd never been.
No longer can those caring folk
Lay wreaths upon their loved ones' graves,
Because the graves are lost to them,
Sunk deep beneath the billowing waves.
The village school has disappeared,
Where children learned and teachers taught;
And blackboards, barnacled and bare,
Stand useless, crumbling, left to rot.
They say that on a stormy night,
When lightning cracks and thunder rolls,
You might just hear a haunting sound
As, eerily, the church bell tolls.

Eileen Hay.

Round Windows

IT'S not so often nowadays
That windows catch one's eye,
Though they come in many sizes
To open up the sky.

In shape they rarely differ,
They are oblong or they're square;
Of all the windows that one sees
There's little to compare.

But a round one is a porthole
That looks far out to sea;
That makes one think of sailing ships
And times that used to be.

Old taverns often had one
Somewhere mysterious, high;
A watch-out place for smugglers
When the Customs men passed by.

So if a house should boast one
It is seen as something rare,
And it might not have a curtain,
But it looks much nicer bare.

And it might be in a belfry
Of an old church with a spire,
Or some unexpected new-build
That is certain to inspire.

There are windows in most houses
Not worth a second glance –
But I'd have "round ones" put in mine
If given half the chance!

Dawn Lawrence.

Autumn Light

LATE autumn, grey and misty –
That early autumn light,
When trees wore glorious colours
And days were crystal bright,
Has faded into drabness
With all the trees now bare,
And days bring misty drizzles
And rawness in the air.
There's something quite nostalgic
About this time of year,
When skies are dark and heavy
And fog forgets to clear.
We resurrect our woollies,
Our winter scarf and hat,
And everyone just scurries –
Too cold to stand and chat.
Our seasons show such contrasts,
Of that there is no doubt;
Without our changing weather
What would we talk about?

Eileen Hay.

The Right Handbag

I HAVE such trials with handbags! They're all too small or wide;
They're far too big for what I need, or things get crammed inside.
The big bags are no good at all; things sink down and get lost.
There are hardly any pockets and they're quite a hefty cost.

The smaller bags look smarter; they're just the kind I seek
To take to all my meetings that I go to every week.
I only need the basics. I haven't got a lot –
And yet there's very little room for the items that I've got!

I need my purse – it's rather fat, it has a job to fit,
And then my lipstick, mirror, too, takes up another bit.
My phone and glasses fill a space, I've notebooks and a pen;
Oh, and then there's hand cream that I need just now and then.

And suddenly, the bag is full, no room to squeeze more in;
No hope of looking elegant with a smaller bag that's thin!
So I have to keep on shopping, in the hope I'll find that prize,
A bag that's big – but not too big – and not too small in size!

Dawn Lawrence.

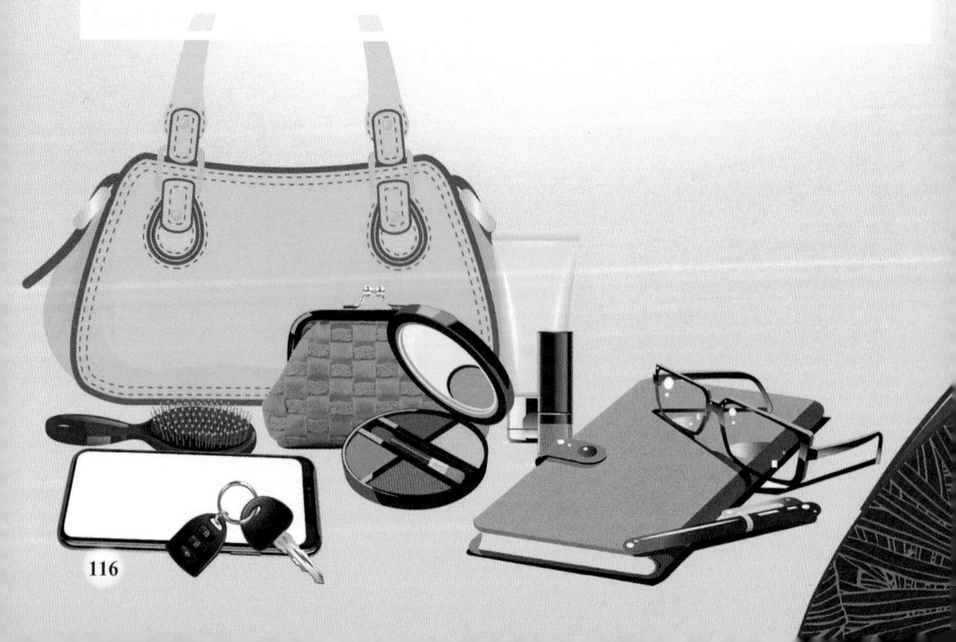

Superstitions

I'M not superstitious, of course I'm not.
Superstitions are funny and quaint!
I do avoid ladders, but that's just because
I might well get all covered in paint!
I do have a horseshoe that hangs on my gate,
And, of course, it is hung the right way
('Cause otherwise all of the luck would run down
And would then simply pour right away!)
One magpie is sad, so I always want two,
And I know broken mirrors aren't good.
Not being superstitious has never harmed me
And, I'm sure, never will – well, touch wood!

Eileen Hay.

from the Manse Window

The Fruit Of Faith

I LOVE the opening line of Keats's poem "To Autumn".

"Season of mists and mellow fruitfulness."

Although it's sad to say goodbye to the summer, there is a glorious beauty to autumn.

I've been fortunate to travel to New England a couple of times in my life, where the autumn colours are spectacular. I love the smell of autumn, the crisp mornings and the golden light at home.

Another thing I love about autumn is the appearance of my favourite apples in the shops – Cox's Orange Pippins and Russets. They taste tart yet sweet, and are crisp to bite into.

We look for the fruit of the year in autumn, the harvest of a season of growing. We expect it to be good and plentiful.

Lately, I've been pondering my fruitfulness as a Christian.

I remember a poster from my youth with a picture of a judge and words written underneath.

If you were accused of being a Christian, would there be enough evidence to convict you?

I doubt it means evidence in terms of going to church, or doing Christian things.

I think it poses the question of whether our lives reflect what we profess to believe.

We live in difficult times when it's tempting to give in to two extremes – either to capitulate to the spirit of the age and accept everything that happens in society without question, or to pull up the drawbridge and resist the changes with a harsh, judgemental attitude.

The hardest challenge is to be faithful to Christian teaching and to reach out in love and compassion without judgement.

People were attracted to Jesus because they knew he would love and accept them.

Of course, he always challenged them to walk away from what was wrong in their lives, but he never let those things stop them from experiencing his love and compassion in the first place.

The disciples, on the other hand, were different. They

by Rev. Susan Sarapuk

didn't want children to bother the teacher who had more important people to deal with.

When a town refused to accept Jesus, they thought he should ask God to rain fire and brimstone down on it.

There was anger and jealousy over who was going to be Jesus's right-hand man when he came into his kingdom.

This is what we do. We want to come out on top – or at least not be at the bottom. We want to be acknowledged; we want to be important.

How many of us have been hurt by the church because we were not recognised or were overlooked?

We want to feel that we are spiritually important and that we mean something to God. Many of us feel we should be doing something great!

Yet Jesus's attitude was totally different. He taught that the kingdom was not about being powerful or having authority in human or religious terms.

iStock.

It's about being a servant, as he demonstrated when he washed the disciples' feet at the Last Supper.

He told his disciples that he was their master and teacher, yet he'd acted as a servant among them. He did not come to be served, but to serve others and to give his life as a ransom for many.

This was so contrary to anything they'd experienced in their religion. Jesus's great disappointment with the Pharisees and scribes was that they were the people who should have been loving and kind, holy and compassionate, instead of rigid and judgemental.

Everything was external – as long as they were seen to be observing the rituals and obeying the rules, they thought they were fine.

But Jesus wanted to do something radical: to make their faith internal; to change people from the inside out.

Sometimes that's the hardest thing for us to understand and put into practice.

Often as Christians we're drawn to the spectacular – somebody exercising the supernatural gifts; a great preacher or worship leader; someone who has authority.

Yes, God is pleased with all these gifts, but chiefly he wants people who are humble; who are servants, and who are like Jesus in their attitudes and lives.

"Take my yoke upon you and learn from me, for I am gentle and humble in heart." (Matt 11:29).

I don't know how much I really want to be gentle and humble in heart because it will involve some sacrifices and difficult decisions at times.

Yet this is what the fruit of faith is all about.

"I can't do it!" maybe you cry with me. That's the point – we can't.

But if we stay close to Jesus, who is the vine and we the branches, if we "abide" in him, then we'll bear much fruit.

Without him we can do nothing – it's just a lot of effort and striving to prove ourselves. I'm praying a lot lately that God will make me fruitful.

I recently bought a cake in the local shop – sponge with a thick lemon icing. When I bit into it, I was expecting the sharp tang of lemon, so imagine my disappointment to find it tasted of absolutely nothing.

It might have gone stale or something could have happened in the manufacturing process, but the only thing I could do was throw it in the bin.

I don't want to be a disappointment to someone who might know about my faith yet see precious little evidence of it in the way I live.

I certainly don't want to be a disappointment to the One who has gone before and set an example that I should follow.

Lord, make me fruitful. ■

Nature's Calendar For Autumn

Like squirrels, jays bury food in the autumn. Tucking away up to 5,000 acorns or hazelnuts, they make sure they're not giving away their position by using bushes or trees to hide. This time of year is the best to see them as they go about collecting food.

As mornings become cooler, it's easier to spot spiders' webs as they're now laced with dew. Spiders have special tiny claws on their legs that help them move across the stickier parts of the web without getting stuck.

Shutterstock.

It's common practice to rake up leaves as soon as they fall, but leaf litter is one of the most nutritious parts of the planet's ecosystem. As it breaks down, it nourishes the soil underneath, and is possibly the biggest contributor to the organic matter in our streams and rivers.

Superblooms occur in desert areas where a large group of wild flowers all burst into flower at once. One of the rarest can be seen occasionally on the Chilean Atacama (the world's driest desert). When the rainfall has been unusually high, the vast plains erupt in an incredible display.

New England is famous for its spectacular display of autumn leaves. It's no wonder, either – there are an estimated 6.5 billion living trees over 32.5 million acres of forest land. There are also 380 million dead trees still standing.

The Fireworks Display

ANTICIPATION in the crowd –
They're merry, laughing, happy, loud!
They just can't wait; it must start soon!
Above, the calm November moon.
A whoosh, a flash, a mighty roar
And suddenly the fireworks soar –
They zoom and flare away up high;
All faces turned towards the sky!
They blaze, they bang, the crowd all cheer
(And parents hold their toddlers near!)
No sparkler ever shone as bright
As children's eyes on Bonfire Night!

Eileen Hay.

All Gone Now

ALL gone now, the men who fought
In the war to end all wars;
And yet, we still remember them
For they embraced a cause.

A cause which has outlived them all,
To keep one's country free,
And to protect the innocent
And honour one's duty.

A duty which they took to heart,
And filled those hearts with pride;
Like those at home who held them dear,
And mourned them when they died.

They died that we might live, we're told,
Their suffering can't be drawn
In words which do them justice
By those who weren't born.

Yet born we were because of those
Who faced adversity.
The triumph of their selflessness –
We live in liberty.

Lynne Hallett.

Nature's Footsteps

AUTUMN has passed with a fanfare,
With trees at their glorious best.
The season turns slowly to winter –
It's time now for nature to rest.

Branches, now free of their foliage,
Are bathed by the clear, falling rain.
Countless small creatures find shelter
And there, for the winter, remain.

Can we follow in nature's footsteps
As autumn slips quietly through,
And take life a little bit easy?
It's time to reflect and renew.

Emma Canning.

The Warmth Of Winter

THE cuckoo has been
And the swallow has gone –
The last days of autumn
Have also moved on.
The days have grown shorter,
But not so the nights,
And the wind, once a whisper,
Now roars as it bites.
We may wish that summer
Could last all year long;
Could wish for warm sunshine
And birds giving song.
But winter can bring us
Its own warmth and light,
When choirs sing sweet carols
And log fires burn bright.
It's that time of year
Which brings folk together
To celebrate Christmas,
Whatever the weather.

John Darley.

Grin And Bear It

WHEN thinking of a winter scene
We picture tranquil snow,
With snowflakes falling gently down
To melt on us below.

But winter can take many forms,
Some raw and dank and grey,
With chills that penetrate our bones
And fog that lasts all day.

Some winter days are sharp and clear
And ears can feel its bite!
The rooftops dangle icicles
That sparkle in the light.

Air feels so cold it hurts our lungs
And brings tears to our eyes,
But nights bring frosty magic, with
Some dazzling starlit skies.

And if we have a snowy spell
With low bright winter sun,
Excited children, woolly warm,
Have lots of sledging fun!

Whatever form our winter takes
We know that we must share it;
And all that you and I can do
Is simply grin and bear it!

Eileen Hay.

A Long Soak

MOST people take showers these days –
It seems that baths are out,
Especially if you're less than fit
Or happen to be stout.
But water pouring on my head
Does not appeal to me;
I much prefer to take a bath
And soak luxuriously.
A lot of bubbles helps, as well,
To soothe those awkward places,
And the mind is kept quite active
With the soap that one misplaces!
A bath, it seems, has qualities
Those showers seem to miss,
Like the art of relaxation,
Warm moments filled with bliss.
But, of course, the main objection
Is when people say they're stout,
And the problem then arises –
They have trouble getting out!

Dawn Lawrence.

SANTA CLAUS
THE NORTH POLE

Christmas Round The Corner

THE months have gone so swiftly by;
The year is fading fast,
But we remember happy days
With memories to last.

November sometimes brings us gloom –
We need a smile or two.
With Christmas round the corner
We've cheerful things to do.

It's time for reaching out to friends
Both near and far away.
For sending loving, caring thoughts,
To warm a chilly day.

A time of looking forward now;
We hope the way is bright.
With Christmas round the corner,
Reach out to love and light.

Iris Hesselden.

Winter White

RED berries of winter on branches,
Crisp frost gleams on bushes and leaves;
The town glistens bright, like sculpture at night
As icicles decorate eaves.
The landscape's become a white painting –
A world that now dazzles our eyes.
Feels like an ice queen has transformed the scene
In a magical, sparkling disguise.
And while it can look so appealing,
We know to take care as we go.
There's always a price – blocked roads and black ice –
Yet we still love white blankets of snow.

Judy Jarvie.

from the Manse Window

Winter Is Coming

MANY people dread the onset of winter not just for the drop in temperature, but also for the increased hours of darkness.

"Now is the winter of our discontent" is the brooding opening line of Shakespeare's "Richard III".

"Winter is coming" is the ominous line repeated in the TV series "Game Of Thrones".

It's bad enough that we feel cold, but short days and long, dark nights seem to add to the potential misery. We think it's bedtime when it's only eight o'clock as it's already been dark for so long.

And having to come out from under the covers to shower and go to work before sunrise? Let's not go there!

The winter or "hibernal" solstice comes when either of the earth's poles is at its maximum tilt away from the sun – December in the northern hemisphere, June in the southern.

With it comes the cold and dark. There's no escaping it.

Now, it's not all bad. Some like to go skiing or ice-skating, while others build snowmen.

Every four years we can enjoy the Winter Olympics, even if many of us will be watching from the warmth of the fireside, armed with a mug of hot tea and the TV remote control!

For those in the north there's a nice irony. Just after midwinter, the time of the longest dark night in December, we have Christmas.

At our darkest point, we get to celebrate the birth of light.

One of the famous Bible passages read in churches worldwide around this time of year is John, Chapter 1, where eyewitness Apostle John makes the dramatic claim that in his friend, Jesus of Nazareth, the Creator has somehow miraculously "become flesh and made his dwelling among us".

The "light" has shone in the "darkness".

There's no doubt the public ministry of Jesus initially sparked high hopes among

by Rev. Andrew Watson

those who encountered him.

The poor and hungry were fed, many who were sick and troubled found healing and peace, and diverse outcasts were included in an eclectic fellowship that was willing to heed his message, turn from wrongdoing and follow this "Son of God".

Of course, darkness need not be in the form of a spectacular stage or TV drama.

It can represent many things for many people: anxiety concerning health or employment, worry over family members or friends, general pessimism about the state of the world and the environment.

We may feel threatened by the words and actions of others, or a measure of sadness and guilt over some of our own.

Well, good news – comfort is available!

The theme of comforting light features again later in John's Gospel, where Jesus says boldly, "I am the light of the world. Whoever follows me will never walk in darkness, but will have the light of life."

This comes just after he has rescued a woman from a crowd threatening to stone her. He has also challenged her to change some aspects of her lifestyle.

One outworking of the distinctive "light" of Jesus is his profound teaching on forgiveness. He graciously forgives us, so we can forgive ourselves and each other and be freed, to live with integrity in the assurance of his love.

Practising what he preached, Jesus taught his followers to "let our light shine" before others, to happily share this experience of his liberating love with everyone.

"Jesus bids us shine then for all around. Many kinds of darkness in this world are found – sin and want and sorrow, so we must shine, you in your small corner and I in mine." So runs the old hymn.

Reflecting Jesus is not without its difficulties. Some people rather like their darkness, have no desire to change and resent being challenged to consider anything different.

Some make a criminal living from abusing others. Many are genuinely confused these days, not sure what is dark or light, wrong or right.

Some need counselling and some need justice. All need the light of the truth and love given by Jesus.

This is where church can be such a positive thing. It's wonderful to know we are not alone.

To be sure, none of us is perfect. We all struggle with different kinds of darkness.

But we don't have to do it unsupported. Together, if we're willing, as a "recovering sinner" we can learn to "walk in the light" of Christ.

In practice, this means trusting and obeying him and loving one another.

I recently watched a short film from Tromsø, Norway, traditionally known as the "land of the midnight sun".

Along with certain other regions north of the Arctic Circle, their peculiar geographical location means for two months each year they have no night, no total darkness.

The sun could be shining brightly at one a.m. You could mow your front lawn or go for a run in relatively clear light in the middle of the night.

It reminded me of something else the Apostle John says near the end of the Bible in the book of Revelation.

Written against a background of cruel persecution in the first century AD, John is given a spectacular and deeply reassuring vision of a coming age when Jesus will return in glory and God will "make all things new".

There will be no more night. They will not need the light of a lamp or the light of the sun, for the Lord God will give them light.

What an encouraging vision for those facing the dark days of winter.

God's light will not be overcome.

These dark days will not last for ever. They will soon pass.

By his grace and kindness we shall be granted to enjoy his perpetual light. ■

iStock.

Nature's Calendar For Winter

The Arctic fox can survive in temperatures as low as -50 deg. C. thanks to its thick winter coat. Once hunted across its homelands, legal protection means the population is now stable.

Icelandic fisherman Gulli Fridporsson survived after his fishing boat capsized in water that was only 5 deg. C. Gulli was overweight, and his body fat was dense in a way similar to seals, which was how he survived the swim and a two-hour walk home in sub-zero temperatures.

Snow isn't a common occurrence in the UK these days, but often it can fall in surprising places! Hawaii, southern Texas and Guadelope have all had dustings, while Rome had nearly a foot in February 2012.

As blackthorn leaves die, the dark-purple sloe berries make themselves obvious in hedgerows and scrubland. They can be used to make jelly, but need to be partnered with an additional source of pectin like cooking apples to help them set.

There's an advantage to trees losing their leaves – it removes another surface for ice and snow to build up on in winter. Conifers fold up their branches towards the trunk to reduce the load, then lower them as the spring comes around.

My View Of The Mountains

I'M missing my view of the mountains.
There is nothing, I know, can compare
With those snow-capped peaks rising to the skies
Like hands clasped in silent prayer.

Yes, I'm missing my view of the mountains,
With clouds slowly drifting above,
And the footpath meandering down through the pines
To the mystical lake I so love.

Where I wake to the song of the skylark
As I open my eyes to dawn's light,
Or dream on beneath a star-spangled sky,
My canopy through every night.

At home, where the rumble of traffic
Is my wakening call for the day,
My mind is bordered on each side by walls
And the stars seem so far, far away.

Yet carved on my heart are those mountains
And the valleys I love to explore.
Mine, all still mine, for the taking
Through memory's wide open door.

Marian Cleworth.

Joined As One

SWIRLING and twirling
On the soft, gentle breeze,
As they fall to the ground,
Brush my cheek with such ease.
Thousands on thousands,
Yet each one unique;
Together, they're strong;
Alone – fragile and weak.

Joining together
Over homes, trees and ground,
Layers of white
Muffling every sound.
Like a sheet freshly laundered,
Laid out crease-free and clean,
Reflecting in lamplight
With a glistening gleam.

Soon the freshness is broken
By prints, large and small,
Entwining and merging
Till another fresh fall.
Breathtaking beauty,
Transformation is done,
Showing what is achieved
When we all join as one.

Amanda-Jayne Lanceley.

Brave Winter Flowers

YOU know it's cold, you know it's grey –
It's a typical bleak winter's day.
But if you take a look around
You'll see that flowers do abound:
The tiny flowers of Springwood White
And Wintersweet – it's pure delight.
Sweet honeysuckle blooms in cold;
Golden Glory, yellow and bold;
Sweet box flowers – a waterfall;
Winter jasmine, bright and small;
Christmas Rose, like pure, white snow –
Brave winter flowers put on a show.

Lily Christie.

A Carpet Of White

NO buses today; no tubes and no trains;
No taxis in London; at airports no planes.
The snow has arrived and on hills once all green
A carpet of white has transformed the whole scene.

Cars move like snails, and ice causes sliding;
Kids on toboggans go hurtling and gliding.
News on TV is all about weather
With pictures and clips and feats of endeavour.

The landscape is iced, a cake-baker's dream –
Snow-covered land like vanilla ice-cream.
As flurries still fall we capture the day
On film, and in hearts, where those memories will stay.

Heather Walker.

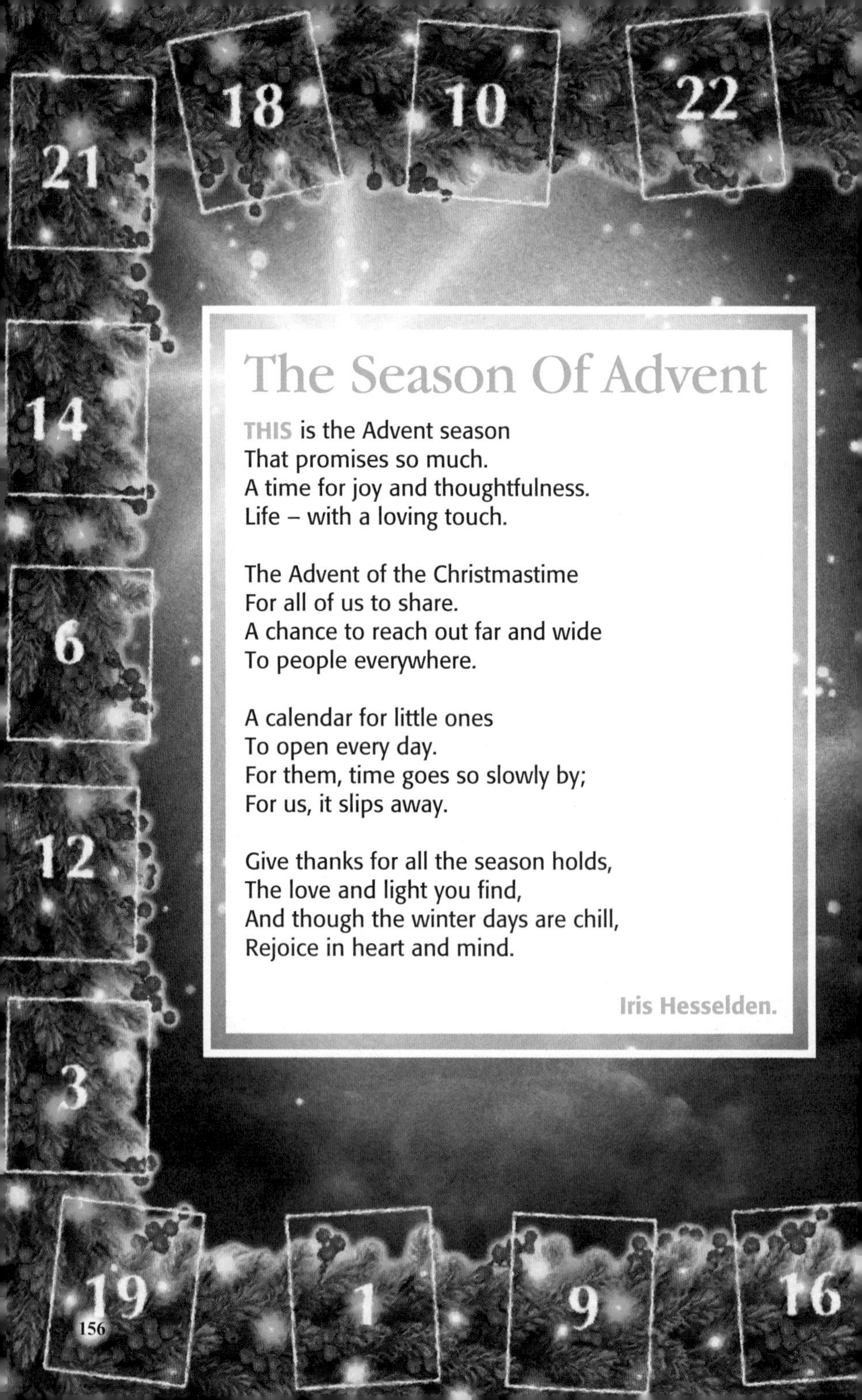

The Season Of Advent

THIS is the Advent season
That promises so much.
A time for joy and thoughtfulness.
Life – with a loving touch.

The Advent of the Christmastime
For all of us to share.
A chance to reach out far and wide
To people everywhere.

A calendar for little ones
To open every day.
For them, time goes so slowly by;
For us, it slips away.

Give thanks for all the season holds,
The love and light you find,
And though the winter days are chill,
Rejoice in heart and mind.

Iris Hesselden.

5
24
13
8
20
17
11
15
7
23

A Christmas Message

THOUGH supermarket Tannoys play
Those tinny carols all day long,
They still have power to touch our hearts
With words that are eternal, strong.

And who, on hearing one brave tot
With hard-brushed hair, and small, scrubbed face,
Sing out a well-loved wavering tune,
Hasn't wiped a teardrop's trace?

Through stained-glass windows, ancient walls,
The joyous voices float above
The frost-rimed, lichen-covered graves
With messages of hope and love.

So, if they're heard in schools or shops
Or in the church on Christmas morn,
The carols' message still rings true –
Our Saviour, Jesus Christ, is born.

Eileen Hay.

All That Glitters

PLEASE don't send me glitter-covered greetings;
Those shiny cards are such an awful trial.
The sparkles drop off in their many thousands
And hide themselves deep in the carpet pile.

They burrow into every nook and cranny,
I find them in the most unusual place,
When I've read your name, with fondest wishes,
They've stuck themselves upon my hand and face.

But if those sparkles catch the evening lamplight
A thousand tiny crystals wink and shine,
Then I see your card is extra special
And I'm sure you'll like the glitter that's on mine!

Elizabeth Brown.

from the Manse Window

Ready Or Not

NO doubt you will remember playing Hide and Seek as children. I always preferred being the one to hide, but if you were to hide you had to be quick.

You only had the time it took the seeker to close his eyes and count to 10, albeit slowly.

Then from your hiding place you would hear the shout of "Coming, ready or not!"

Sometimes you were still dithering about where to hide when it got to 10, making you an easy target to catch.

Then it became your turn to be the seeker.

Seeking was a tedious and somewhat exhausting job, searching in all the usual places, trying to have eyes in the back of your head, darting here and there as children popped out when your back was turned and made it back to home base.

"Coming, ready or not" is a very good phrase as we approach the season leading up to Christmas.

Christmas will come with all its fanfare of blaring carols and jingles, hectic shopping, sparkling light displays for indoors and outdoors – and stress!

"Are you ready for Christmas? Have you done all your shopping?" is the usual greeting on the streets.

Shopkeepers will have been preparing since the end of August.

Summer sales will have emptied the racks and the Christmas look will be taking shape.

The shops will be ready for all our money with enticing new Christmas displays, new decorations, new toys and the newest of must-have gifts.

Farmers will be ready with turkeys and chickens, butchers with lovely joints of meat, florists with cyclamen and poinsettias. Christmas trees will be felled and Brussels sprouts will make a big comeback.

Whether or not you have forgotten the crackers or the stuffing, or to post the mail to Australia in time, will be immaterial. Christmas will have come whether you are

iStock.

by Janice Ross

ready or not.

Then it will be Boxing Day, for some a day to lie around in front of the TV and to finish off the leftover turkey; for others a brisk walk to walk off all the over-indulgence of the day before.

Our bins will be full to overflowing with torn Christmas wrapping-paper and there will be a slight feeling of relief or disappointment that it has come and gone, depending on our age.

Do I sound a bit cynical, or is that a fair description of Christmas for many in our country these days?

The question is "Are we ready for Jesus coming?", which, after all, is what Advent and Christmas are all about.

Perhaps we have not even considered him. Many people simply leave Jesus out of Christmas altogether.

"What has Jesus got to do with Christmas?" a young mum asked a friend of mine recently in all seriousness.

I personally remember, as long ago as 1969, taking part in a student march in Edinburgh under the banner "Put Christ back into Christmas".

For 400 years there had been a period of silence for the Jewish nation. There were no more messages from God through the prophets.

iStock.

Many forgot the words passed down by their forefathers and lost interest in the God of Abraham, Isaac and Jacob.

But there were those who were faithful and who continued to hold on to the hope that one day a Messiah would come. They were ready and anxious for his coming.

The first mentioned in Luke's gospel is Elizabeth, the wife of Zechariah and cousin of Mary. Miraculously she and Zechariah were expecting a child in their old age.

We are told that when Mary entered her home to share her astonishing news, Elizabeth's own baby leaped in her womb in such a way that Elizabeth knew she was in the presence of the Messiah.

"But why am I so favoured that the mother of my Lord should come to me?"

What an encouragement she must have been to the young and vulnerable Mary.

Eight days after his birth Jesus was taken by his parents to the temple, as was the tradition. There, we are told, the little family met a good and righteous man called Simeon.

He, too, had been waiting for "the consolation of Israel". The Holy Spirit had told him he wouldn't die before he had seen the Lord's Christ.

He felt prompted to visit the temple at just the time Mary and Joseph came to present their son.

Simeon praised God with the words, "For my eyes have seen your salvation" and gave the parents a prophetic word that their little son would be a blessing to both Jew and Gentile.

Soon an old lady joined them. Anna was a prophetess who worshipped and prayed day and night in the temple.

She, too, recognised the child as the One she had been waiting for, and with great joy passed on the news to all who were waiting for the Messiah who would bring redemption to Jerusalem.

Although we like to imagine the Wise Men from the East making up the Christmas tableau, their arrival was believed to be some time later. These distinguished foreigners had paid particular attention to a new star which had guided them to the baby Jesus.

"Where is the child who has been born King of the Jews?" they asked.

When they found him they bowed in worship and presented him with gifts of gold, frankincense and myrrh.

At Christmas we remember with joy and gratitude that Jesus offers to come again to any who are waiting for a Saviour and Redeemer.

He is no longer a baby. He is no longer just a man, but God's Son, who died and rose again.He is coming once again to offer eternal life to all who are ready and waiting. ■

Nature's Calendar For Winter

The metabolism of aquatic turtles slows during winter – at anything below 10 deg. C. – so they can conserve energy while they hibernate. During this time they absorb oxygen through their skin to breathe.

The stunning Mendenhall Glacier has some of the bluest ice caverns in the world. In these frosty spaces carved by water, there's often mist floating around the floor and small waterfalls within. It's in Alaska, but is retreating with global warming.

Shutterstock.

Niagara Falls carries so much water that it's nearly impossible for it to freeze – unless it freezes further upstream and reduces the flow of water – but there were two polar vortex events in 2014 and 2015 when the extreme cold made it appear that it almost had.

About 40 to 50 people overwinter on the Amundsen-Scott South Pole Station, just a stone's throw from the pole. The last flight out leaves mid to late February, and the first flight back is usually in October. In between, planes don't fly that far south as there's a strong risk that their fuel will freeze.

Inuit culture is famous for having 50 words for the different kinds of snow they experience, but the Scots can top that. There are supposedly 100 words for rain in Scots, from daggle (falling in torrents) to smirr (a fine drizzle).

Mary's Child

WHO is this child whose gaze holds mine
And fills my heart with awe,
Whom shepherds view upon their knees
And wise men bow before?

Who is this child with eyes so wise
That silently portend
Some pre-determined destiny
I cannot comprehend?

Who is this child whose stare can leave
My mind in disarray,
Unmasking every frailty
Till I must look away?

Who is this child I carried long,
A stranger now to me,
Whose inner wisdom radiates
From depths I cannot see?

Who is this child I thought was mine,
This child that I adore,
Who fate decrees must save mankind?
Once mine, but mine no more.

Sylvia Smith.

The True Spirit Of Christmas

THE snow, a pure white blanket,
Lays softly on the earth,
And bells are rung and carols sung
To celebrate his birth.

Let's hope the festive spirit
Retains its Christmas cheer,
So peace, goodwill, is with us still
Throughout the coming year.

John Darley.

Fleeting Time

HOW very strange is fleeting time
And how it slips away,
The weeks and months all disappear
As swiftly as a day.

But then there are those other times
When hours drag their feet,
When we are missing someone dear
And long once more to meet.

For children, Christmas takes so long,
And Guy Fawkes Night, the same.
They have to wait for birthdays, too,
It really seems a shame!

But then, as we grow older,
The year goes rushing on,
The spring and summer light our lives,
Then suddenly they're gone.

But time is precious; life's a gift
To cherish, come what may.
Enjoy the wonder in the world
And always seize the day!

Iris Hesselden.

"The most I can do for my friend is simply be his friend."
– *Henry David Thoreau*